BEST OF THE SUPER BOWL

SURPRISE SUPER BOWL HEROES

BY DAVID J. CLARKE

SportsZone

An Imprint of Abdo Publishing
abdobooks.com

abdobooks.com

Published by Abdo Publishing, a division of ABDO, PO Box 398166, Minneapolis, Minnesota 55439.

Printed in the United States of America, North Mankato, Minnesota.
102024
012025

THIS BOOK CONTAINS RECYCLED MATERIALS

Cover Photos: Focus On Sport/Getty Images Sport/Getty Images (left); George Rose/Getty Images Sport/Getty Images (middle); Kevin C. Cox/Getty Images Sport/Getty Images (right)
Interior Photos: Tony Tomsic/AP Images, 4, 36; Focus On Sport/Getty Images, 6, 16, 19, 26; Focus On Sport/Getty Images Sport/Getty Images, 9, 29; Rich Pilling/Sporting News Archive/Getty Images, 11; Jamie Squire/Getty Images Sport/Getty Images, 12, 33; Timothy A. Clary/AFP/Getty Images, 15, 22, 31; Carmen Mandato/Getty Images Sport/Getty Images, 20; Rich Kane/Icon SMI/Corbis/Icon Sportswire/Getty Images, 25; Ezra Shaw/Getty Images Sport/Getty Images, 35; Brian Bahr/Getty Images Sport/Getty Images, 39; Paul Spinelli/AP Images, 41; Ronald Martinez/Getty Images Sport/Getty Images, 43; George Rose/Getty Images Sport/Getty Images, 44; Jed Jacobsohn/Getty Images Sport/Getty Images, 45

Editor: Charlie Beattie
Series Designer: Jake Slavik

Library of Congress Control Number: 2024938338

Publisher's Cataloging-in-Publication Data

Names: Clarke, David J., author.
Title: Surprise Super Bowl heroes / by David J. Clarke
Description: Minneapolis, Minnesota: ABDO Publishing, 2025 | Series: Best of the Super Bowl | Includes online resources and index.
Identifiers: ISBN 9781098295448 (lib. bdg.) | ISBN 9798384916444 (ebook)
Subjects: LCSH: Super Bowl--Records--Juvenile literature. | American football--Juvenile literature. | National Football League--Juvenile literature. | Football--United States--History--Juvenile literature.
Classification: DDC 796.332648--dc23

TABLE OF CONTENTS

CHAPTER ONE
UNSUNG OFFENSE 4

CHAPTER TWO
DEFENSIVE DYNAMOS 16

CHAPTER THREE
SUPER SPECIAL TEAMS 26

CHAPTER FOUR
ONE-PLAY WONDERS 36

HONORABLE MENTIONS 44
GLOSSARY 46
MORE INFORMATION 47
ONLINE RESOURCES 47
INDEX 48
ABOUT THE AUTHOR 48

CHAPTER ONE

UNSUNG OFFENSE

Max McGee didn't expect to play much in Super Bowl I. The Green Bay Packers wide receiver backed up Boyd Dowler, who was one of the best pass catchers in the National Football League (NFL). But when Dowler injured his shoulder early in the game on January 15, 1967, McGee went in.

He wasn't in the best of shape. Since he didn't think he would play, McGee had broken the team curfew and stayed out late the night before. But with 6:35 left in the first quarter, McGee broke down the middle of the field. Quarterback Bart Starr's pass was behind the 34-year-old receiver. McGee reached his right hand back to pull it in and raced to the end zone for the first touchdown in Super Bowl history. It was just McGee's fifth catch of the season. He would finish

Seven of Max McGee's 12 career playoff receptions came in Super Bowl I.

the game with seven receptions for 138 yards. McGee also caught another touchdown pass.

SNELL STEPS UP

Heading into Super Bowl III in January 1969, much of the talk around the New York Jets surrounded their quarterback. Joe Namath had predicted his underdog team would beat the Baltimore Colts. Few believed him. Even his own teammates weren't thrilled with "Broadway Joe's" boast.

Matt Snell, *right*, plows across the goal line for the Jets' only touchdown of Super Bowl III.

One of those teammates was Matt Snell, the team's star running back. Snell had rushed for more than 700 yards during the regular season. He added 71 more in the team's 27–23 victory over the Oakland Raiders in the American Football League (AFL) playoffs to reach the Super Bowl. But with all the hype around Namath, no one was talking about Snell.

On a muddy Super Bowl Sunday in Miami, both teams struggled to score. The game was still 0–0 when the Jets took over at their own 20 with 14:09 remaining in the second quarter. They put together a 12-play scoring drive. Snell touched the ball on seven of them. He finished it off with a 4-yard touchdown run.

It was New York's only touchdown in a 16–7 upset victory. Snell finished the game with 30 carries for 121 yards. He also grabbed four passes for 40 yards. The game's Most Valuable Player (MVP) Award went to Namath. But the victory would not have been possible without Snell.

PLUNKETT'S COMEBACKS

Not many teams wanted quarterback Jim Plunkett in the summer of 1978. He had spent seven seasons playing for bad teams in New England and San Francisco. Plunkett was so beaten up from taking sacks over the years that he could barely suit up.

However, the Oakland Raiders took him in. Two years later, when starting quarterback Dan Pastorini was injured during the regular season, Plunkett took over. He led the Raiders all the way to Super Bowl XV. There, he threw three touchdown passes in a 27–10 win over the Philadelphia Eagles. The unlikely hero was named the game's MVP.

By the 1983 season, Plunkett was once again a backup. And the Raiders had moved to Los Angeles. However, when starter Marc Wilson was hurt, Plunkett got his job back. He followed the same script as the 1980 season. In the end, Plunkett led the Raiders back to the Super Bowl, where they routed Washington 38–9. Plunkett's numbers weren't as good as the first time around. But he still threw for 172 yards and a score. With that victory, Plunkett became the fifth quarterback to win the Super Bowl two times. The other four were Hall of Famers Terry Bradshaw, Bob Griese, Starr, and Roger Staubach. Four decades later, Plunkett still had not joined them.

THREE SURPRISES

When Denver faced Washington in Super Bowl XXII after the 1987 season, the Broncos coaches probably didn't spend much time game-planning for quarterback Doug Williams, running back Timmy Smith, and receiver Ricky Sanders. Smith, a rookie, had barely played all year. Williams started a handful of games during the regular season but didn't get the job full time until the playoffs. And Sanders was buried on the depth chart behind star pass catchers Art Monk and Gary Clark.

Jim Plunkett looks for an open receiver during the Raiders' 27–10 victory over the Philadelphia Eagles in Super Bowl XV.

TAYLOR'S MOMENT

San Francisco 49ers superstar wide receiver Jerry Rice had a record-setting day in Super Bowl XXIII in January 1989. He caught every pass Joe Montana had to offer and finished with 11 grabs for 215 yards and a touchdown. San Francisco's other wideout, John Taylor, caught only one pass in the game. But it was a big one. With 34 seconds left, he caught a 10-yard strike for the winning score in the 49ers' 20–16 victory over the Cincinnati Bengals.

However, as Washington exploded for 35 second-quarter points, all three unsung heroes were front and center. On the team's first play of the quarter, Williams hit Sanders for an 80-yard touchdown pass. On Washington's next drive, Smith ran for 20 yards before Williams threw another touchdown pass to put his team up 14–10.

When Washington got the ball back, it faced first-and-10 from its own 42-yard line. Smith took a handoff and broke to the right sideline. As two Broncos tried to chase him down, he broke free for a 58-yard score.

Sanders cemented his Super Bowl legend by catching a 50-yard touchdown pass on the next drive. The final score of the game was 42–10. Williams had set a Super Bowl record with 340 passing yards while throwing four touchdowns. Smith's 204 rushing yards made him the first running back to break 200 yards. Sanders also had a record-smashing day, catching nine

Ricky Sanders races for an 80-yard touchdown in the second quarter of Super Bowl XXII.

passes for 193 yards and two scores. While only Smith's record still stands, the trio's performance will never be forgotten.

WHITE FOR THE WIN

Super Bowl LI in February 2017 is best-remembered for the New England Patriots' 25-point comeback to defeat the Atlanta Falcons

James White was a member of three championship teams during his eight seasons with the Patriots.

34–28 in overtime. New England's legendary quarterback Tom Brady broke Super Bowl records for completions (42), pass attempts (63), and passing yards (466). After the game, Brady was given a pickup truck for winning the game's MVP Award. Brady felt he didn't deserve either. While he couldn't give away the award, he gifted the truck to the player he truly felt should have been honored.

Patriots running back James White shared running duties with two other backs during the season. But in the Super Bowl, White was spectacular. He caught a record 14 passes for 110 yards and a touchdown. However, his two biggest plays came on the ground. New England still trailed 28–20 with 57 seconds left when White plunged in from one yard out. It was his first rushing touchdown of the entire season.

After a two-point conversion tied the game, the teams went to the extra period. Brady led New England down the field to the Atlanta 2-yard line. From there, White barreled over the goal line for the winning score. When it was all over, Brady had the MVP hardware, but White went home with the truck.

FOLES FILLS IN

Nick Foles began his career with the Philadelphia Eagles in 2012. But after three years with the team, he was traded away in 2015. Two years later, new Eagles head coach Doug Pederson brought Foles back to Philadelphia. But this time, Foles would not be the starter. The quarterback's job was to sit on the bench and support the team's young star, Carson Wentz.

However, Wentz severely injured his knee late in the 2017 season. The Eagles were 11–2 when Wentz was hurt, but suddenly the season looked like it could be a disappointment. However, Foles took over and kept the team rolling through the playoffs. When the Eagles reached Minneapolis for Super Bowl LII, it was the journeyman Foles against New England's Brady, the greatest Super Bowl quarterback of all time.

Brady broke his one-year-old record for passing yards in a Super Bowl. He diced the Eagles secondary for 505 yards through the air. But Foles stayed with the legend pass for pass. He threw for 373 yards and three scores. Foles then did Brady one better by catching a touchdown pass on a trick play late in the first half.

The Patriots took their only lead 33–32 with 9:22 left in the game. But Foles led a masterful 14-play drive over the next seven minutes. With 2:21 left, he tossed a touchdown pass to tight end Zach Ertz for the winning score. The Eagles won the game 41–33. And Foles left Minneapolis as the Super Bowl's latest unlikely hero.

Nick Foles was named the MVP of Super Bowl LII.

CHAPTER TWO

DEFENSIVE DYNAMOS

Defensive players don't often get as much attention as stars on offense. Since they rarely touch the ball, it can be tougher to get noticed. Often in big games like the Super Bowl, an offensive player gets the MVP Award. But it takes a great defense to win the game. The Dallas Cowboys proved that more than once in the 1970s.

The Cowboys' feared "Doomsday Defense" helped the team reach five Super Bowls during the decade. In Super Bowl V after the 1970 season, Cowboys linebacker Chuck Howley won MVP honors. And his team hadn't even won the game. It was the first time the award had gone to a player on the losing team.

The Cowboys produced another MVP "first" later in the decade. The team squared off with the Denver Broncos in Super Bowl XII in January 1978. Dallas brought a fearsome front four of Harvey Martin,

Harvey Martin was the NFL's Defensive Player of the Year during the 1977 season.

Randy White, Ed "Too Tall" Jones, and Jethro Pugh. The quartet made life miserable for Denver quarterback Craig Morton. The Cowboys' punishing hits forced Morton into several mistakes. He was eventually pulled from the game in the third quarter. Dallas then teed off on Denver backup Norris Weese.

In the end, the Cowboys ran out to a 27–10 victory. Martin finished with two sacks while White had one. Both players shared the MVP Award. It was the first time it had ever been given out to multiple players.

PICK THREE

Linebacker Rod Martin was a two-time Pro Bowl player during his 12 years with the Oakland/Los Angeles Raiders. So if the team was going to upset the favored Philadelphia Eagles in Super Bowl XV after the 1980 season, the 26-year-old would have to make an impact. However, how Martin did that surprised everyone.

Martin had been a 12th-round draft pick out of college in 1977. Few expected he would be a star, or even last in the NFL. At 218 pounds, some thought he was too small to play linebacker, but too big to play defensive back. Super Bowl XV was one of the many times he proved his doubters wrong.

On the third play of the game, Eagles quarterback Ron Jaworski dropped back and tossed a pass toward the left sideline intended for tight end John Spagnola. Martin jumped in the passing lane and

Rod Martin holds up three fingers to the crowd, one for each of his interceptions in Super Bowl XV.

BOLTON FINDS PAY DIRT

The Kansas City Chiefs trailed the Philadelphia Eagles 14–7 in the second quarter of Super Bowl LVII in February 2023. Then, Chiefs linebacker Nick Bolton scooped up a fumble and raced 36 yards for a tying score. Bolton nearly did it again in the third quarter. He picked up a fumble and sprinted 24 yards to the end zone. However, an official review of the play changed the call from a fumble to an incomplete pass.

picked it off. His 17-yard interception return set up the team's first score.

That would have been a great highlight for a linebacker with just two career interceptions to that point. But Martin was far from done. The Raiders led 21–3 with just under nine minutes left in the third quarter when Martin picked Jaworski again. This time, Martin's interception set up a field goal.

Oakland built its lead to 27–10 with 3:01 left. There was still time for Martin to ensure he walked away as the game's MVP. When Jaworski heaved a desperate pass over the middle of the field, Martin swooped in for his record third interception.

Martin played in the NFL until 1988. He retired as a Raiders legend. In 1983, United Press International named him the defensive player of the year. But his most famous moment remains his incredible performance in Super Bowl XV.

LARRY BROWN'S BIG MOMENT

The Dallas Cowboys were gearing up for their third Super Bowl in four years in January 1996. In the buildup, few fans were paying attention to Dallas cornerback Larry Brown. Most of the talk was about the team's other corner, Deion "Prime Time" Sanders.

Sanders attracted attention for his gold chains, his big mouth, and his spectacular play. Quarterbacks were afraid to even throw his direction. Not surprisingly, Pittsburgh Steelers quarterback Neil O'Donnell spent most of Super Bowl XXX tossing passes to the other side of the field. The result was two easy interceptions for Brown. Both led to Dallas scores in a 27–17 Cowboys victory.

Brown was named the game's MVP. In the offseason, he turned his big night into big dollars. He signed a five-year $12.5 million contract with the Oakland Raiders. But Brown never lived up to the deal. He was out of Oakland within two seasons.

TAMPA BAY PICK PARTY

Everyone knew the Oakland Raiders would put the ball in the air heading into Super Bowl XXXVII after the 2002 season. Their quarterback, Rich Gannon, had led the league in passing yards during the regular season. Gannon was the NFL MVP that year, but the Tampa Bay Buccaneers were ready.

The season before, Tampa Bay coach Jon Gruden had coached Gannon in Oakland. In an odd move, the Raiders had actually traded

Dwight Smith (26) outraces Oakland Raiders quarterback Rich Gannon for a touchdown during Super Bowl XXXVII.

the coach to Tampa Bay before the season. Gruden wanted revenge on his old team. And he knew the Raiders' playbook by heart.

The Raiders took an early 3–0 lead. But Tampa Bay scored the next 34 points. A big reason why was the play of the Buccaneers' pass defense. During that run, free safety Dexter Jackson intercepted Gannon twice. The final touchdown in the scoring spree came on a 44-yard interception return by cornerback Dwight Smith.

The Buccaneers were far from done ruining Gannon's day. With the score 34–21 and 1:18 left, Derrick Brooks picked off another pass. The star linebacker raced 44 yards down the sideline for a touchdown.

The game was decided at that point. But Gannon tried to throw again. Smith punished the mistake by intercepting a tipped pass and racing 50 yards to the end zone. He became the first player to score two defensive touchdowns in the same Super Bowl. But Jackson was named the game's MVP.

MVP MALCOLM

The 2013 Seattle Seahawks boasted a punishing defense. The team's hard-hitting secondary was nicknamed the "Legion of Boom." In front of them, standout linebackers Bobby Wagner and K. J. Wright stuffed opposing rushers.

Seattle's third linebacker was a former seventh-round draft pick named Malcolm Smith. The 2013 season was Smith's first as a starter. He quietly finished fifth on the team in tackles. But the young linebacker had made a name for himself in the playoffs. Late in the National Football Conference (NFC) Championship Game, Smith intercepted a San Francisco 49ers' pass in the end zone. The play sealed a 23–17 Seattle win.

That set up a matchup with the Denver Broncos in Super Bowl XLVIII. Smith was all over the field in the game. He finished tied for the team high with 10 tackles. But he also made two highlight-reel plays.

Late in the second quarter, the Seahawks held a 15–0 lead. But the Broncos were driving. On third-and-13 from the Seattle 35, Denver quarterback Peyton Manning tried to throw to the right side. His arm was hit on the play, and the ball dropped to Smith at the 31-yard line. With his defensive line forming a blocking wall, Smith sprinted 69 yards for the score.

With 6:08 remaining in the third quarter, Manning hit wide receiver Demaryius Thomas on a deep pass. But Seattle cornerback Byron Maxwell forced the ball out, and Smith recovered the fumble. Seattle's offense then took the ball 58 yards for a touchdown to make it 29–0. In the end, the Seahawks walked away with their first championship in a blowout 43–8 win. And the MVP of the game was the formerly unknown Smith.

Seattle linebacker Malcolm Smith tries to avoid a Denver Broncos' tackler after recovering a fumble in Super Bowl XLVIII.

CHAPTER THREE

SUPER SPECIAL TEAMS

Super Bowl V in January 1971 was not a pretty game to watch. The Dallas Cowboys and Baltimore Colts combined for a Super Bowl–low 24 first downs in the game. Five of those were earned through penalties. The three quarterbacks who played in the game combined for six interceptions.

Despite the poor play, the game came down to an exciting finish. The score was tied 13–13 with just over one minute to play. Then Colts linebacker Mike Curtis picked off Dallas quarterback Craig Morton and ran the ball 13 yards to the Dallas 28.

The Colts' offense only had to move the ball into position for a game-winning field goal. Three plays and three yards later, kicker Jim O'Brien trotted out with a chance to be a Super Bowl hero.

Jim O'Brien, *right*, celebrates his game-winning kick in Super Bowl V with quarterback Earl Morrall.

O'Brien's only other kick in the game had been blocked. With his helmet chinstrap unbuttoned, the rookie booted a 32-yarder through the uprights for a 16–13 lead. The Colts sealed their win two plays later when they intercepted Morton again. O'Brien played just four years in the NFL. But he remains an important part of the league's history as the first kicker to boot a Super Bowl–winning field goal in the last minute of the game.

DESMOND DAZZLES

Desmond Howard was a household name for football fans well before he entered the NFL in 1992. A year earlier, the wide receiver and return specialist had won the Heisman Trophy as the best player in college football while at the University of Michigan. Washington had made him the fourth overall pick in the 1992 draft.

Howard struggled in the NFL, however. He played three disappointing seasons in Washington before being picked in the 1995 expansion draft by the Jacksonville Jaguars. Howard spent only one season in Florida.

In the summer of 1996, the Green Bay Packers picked Howard up. The team didn't need him to be a pass catcher. But Howard's speed and shifty moves made him a great kick returner. Howard brought back three punts for touchdowns during the season. The Packers raced all the way to a Super Bowl XXXI matchup with the New England Patriots.

Desmond Howard's touchdown in Super Bowl XXXI was the only kickoff return touchdown of his career.

Green Bay was a big favorite to win the game. But with just over three minutes left in the third quarter, an 18-yard touchdown run by New England running back Curtis Martin cut the Packers' lead to 27–21. Green Bay needed a spark in the suddenly tight game.

Howard had been waiting for his moment all evening. After a 31-yard punt return in the first quarter, he shouted at the

New England bench. Howard spent the rest of the game verbally sparring with Patriots' players. But the Packers' return man got the last laugh. After the Martin touchdown, he took kicker Adam Vinatieri's boot at the 1-yard line. Spotting a gap up the middle, Howard took off. Only one Patriot got a hand on him as Howard raced 99 yards for the score.

The final score of the game was 35–21. Howard racked up 244 yards, all on returns. And his 99-yard runback put the finishing touch on Green Bay's first Super Bowl win in 29 years. After the game, Howard was named Super Bowl MVP. He was the first special teams player ever to win the award.

VICTORIOUS VINATIERI

Vinatieri retired from the NFL in 2019 as a five-time Super Bowl winner and the league's all-time leading scorer. He is considered one of the best ever at his position. But entering Super Bowl XXXVI in February 2002, few NFL fans outside of New England knew who he was.

Vinatieri grew up in South Dakota and attended South Dakota State University, a school not known for producing pro athletes. Unsurprisingly, NFL teams ignored him coming out of college. He ended up kicking for a team in Amsterdam, Netherlands, in the spring of 1996 while he waited for a chance. The Patriots snapped him up in July of that year.

Adam Vinatieri, *left*, jumps into the arms of holder Ken Walter after hitting the game-winning field goal in Super Bowl XXXVI.

In the 2001 season, a then little-known quarterback named Tom Brady led New England on a surprise run to Super Bowl XXXVI. By then, Vinatieri was 29 years old. That year, he had made 24 of 30 field goal attempts. But all of his misses had come outdoors. Since the

Super Bowl was being played indoors at the Superdome in New Orleans, the Patriots knew they had a weapon. With 8 seconds left, they unleashed it. With the Patriots and the favored St. Louis Rams tied 17–17, New England lined up for a 48-yard field goal. Everyone wearing Patriots blue was confident. Long snapper Lonie Paxton knew Vinatieri was "automatic." Offensive coordinator Charlie Weis was so sure Vinatieri would make it that he started to look for his kids in the stands. That way he could wave them down onto the field for the celebration.

Sure enough, Vinatieri delivered. His boot split the uprights to win the game 20–17. It was New England's first title. And overnight, Vinatieri was known from one end of the country to the other.

JONES TURNS THE LIGHTS OUT

Super Bowl XLVII was billed as the "Harbaugh Bowl." San Francisco 49ers head coach Jim Harbaugh was set to face his brother John Harbaugh, the head coach of the Baltimore Ravens. By the time it was over, the game was more famous for the blackout that shut the lights off in New Orleans' Superdome for more than 30 minutes in the third quarter. But before the lights went out, Baltimore receiver Jacoby Jones stole the show.

The 28-year-old Jones was a steady receiver. But he was dangerous as a return man. During the regular season, he had run back two kickoffs and one punt for touchdowns.

The meeting of brothers Jim, *right*, and John Harbaugh was a big story leading up to Super Bowl XLVII. But it was soon overshadowed by the incredible on-field events.

Jones first made his mark on offense. With 1:45 left in the second quarter, he hauled in a 56-yard touchdown pass from quarterback Joe Flacco. The score put the Ravens up 21–3.

It was 21–6 when the teams came out for the second half. Jones is a native of Louisiana. He was excited to be playing at home. But he saved his biggest thrill for the start of the third quarter.

Before the game, Jones had warned the 49ers not to kick to him. San Francisco kicker David Akers sent the third-quarter kickoff high and deep. Jones caught it while standing near the back of his own end zone. In that situation, most players would catch the ball and kneel for a touchback. But Jones grabbed it and started out. Using his long strides, the 6-foot, 3-inch return man blew through a hole in the middle of the field. He exploded past San Francisco's defenders and raced to the end zone to make it 28–6. It proved to be a key play in the game. The Ravens were able to withstand a San Francisco rally. The final score was Baltimore 34, San Francisco 31.

FREE COUCH

Without knowing it, Jacoby Jones earned a lot of people in the Baltimore area free furniture with his kick return. A local store told shoppers that all items purchased between the Wednesday before the Super Bowl and game day were free if a Ravens player returned a kick for a score. When Jones did it, the store honored its promise. It gave out roughly $600,000 in refunds.

Jacoby Jones (12) races away from a pack of San Francisco 49ers' defenders on his way to his record-setting return in Super Bowl XLVII.

Jones's runback was originally ruled a 109-yard return. That would have tied an NFL record for the longest play in league history. Later, an official review of the play shortened it to 108 yards. Jones had to settle for the NFL's postseason record instead.

24
68

CHAPTER FOUR

ONE-PLAY WONDERS

By the 1976 season, the Oakland Raiders were frustrated. The team had lost Super Bowl II to the Green Bay Packers after the 1967 season. Every year since, Oakland was in contention. But the team fell short in each of the six AFC title games it reached over the next eight years.

The Raiders finally broke through to face the Minnesota Vikings in Super Bowl XI in January 1977. One of the team's relieved veterans was cornerback Willie Brown. The future Hall of Famer had been with the Raiders since 1967. The now 36-year-old Brown was eager to finally win a title.

With just over six minutes left in the game, Oakland led the Vikings 26–7. Minnesota quarterback Fran Tarkenton had guided the team to the Raiders 28, hoping for a miracle comeback. But on

Willie Brown races down the field for his game-sealing interception in Super Bowl XI.

first-and-10, Brown cut in front of Minnesota receiver Sammy White at the 25 and intercepted Tarkenton's pass.

Brown had clear daylight to the end zone to seal the win. As he sprinted to paydirt, Oakland radio announcer Bill King screamed "He's going all the way! Old Man Willie! Touchdown Raiders!" King's unfortunate nickname stuck with Brown for the rest of his life. But so did the Super Bowl ring he earned for Oakland's 32–14 win.

VRABEL AT THE GOAL LINE

Mike Vrabel was a solid linebacker for the New England Patriots from 2001 to 2008. He helped the team win three Super Bowls. And Vrabel also occasionally pitched in on offense.

With under three minutes to play in Super Bowl XXXVIII in February 2004, the Patriots trailed the Carolina Panthers 22–21. On second-and-goal from the Carolina 2-yard line, Vrabel snuck onto the field as an extra tight end. Quarterback Tom Brady dropped back to pass and fired a hard pass that Vrabel snagged for the go-ahead score. Vrabel was the first defensive player to score an offensive touchdown in the game since Super Bowl XX nearly 20 years earlier. New England went on to win 32–29.

A year later, New England was facing the Philadelphia Eagles in Super Bowl XXXIX. The score was tied 7–7 early in the third quarter. Once again the Patriots marched to the opposing goal line. Needing two yards to score, Vrabel lined up at tight end on the left side of

Mike Vrabel hangs on for a touchdown against the Philadelphia Eagles in Super Bowl XXXIX.

the line. He exploded off the ball. Eagles defensive end Jevon Kearse grabbed a hunk of Vrabel's jersey. Still, Brady lobbed a pass that direction. With Kearse holding on, Vrabel tipped the ball, then caught it for the go-ahead score. It proved to be a key play in a 24–21 win.

THE HELMET CATCH

Entering Super Bowl XLII in January 2008, all eyes were on the New England Patriots. The team was 18–0 entering the game. The Patriots were trying to become the first perfect champions since 1972.

The New York Giants were heavy underdogs. But they trailed just 14–10 in the final moments and had the ball. On third-and-five from their own 44-yard line, New York quarterback Eli Manning dropped back to pass. He escaped pressure, then fired a desperate heave down the middle of the field. Both Giants receiver David Tyree and New England safety Rodney Harrison jumped for the ball at the same time. Tyree got his hands on it, and as the two players fell, Harrison tried to rip it out. Tyree managed to hold the ball by pinning it with his fingertips to his helmet.

Tyree was an unknown player entering the game. He had caught four passes all season. But he had snagged a five-yard touchdown pass earlier in the game to introduce himself to football fans. Certainly no one could forget him after the incredible "helmet catch." Especially after the Giants later scored to finish off a historic 17–14 upset.

In 2017, the NFL named David Tyree's "Helmet Catch" the top play in Super Bowl history.

AMBUSH

Coming out of halftime at Super Bowl XLIV in February 2010, the New Orleans Saints needed a jolt. The team trailed the Indianapolis Colts 10–6 after a tough first half. New Orleans head coach Sean Payton decided to gamble.

The Saints were kicking off to start the third quarter. But instead of booting the ball deep, Payton wanted an onside kick. When told of the plan, Saints kicker Thomas Morstead said he was "terrified." If it went wrong, the Colts would have the ball and a short distance to the end zone.

The play was called "Ambush" in the Saints' playbook. Worried or not, Morstead sent a perfect bouncing ball toward the left sideline. The shocked Colts had a chance to recover but bobbled it. After a scramble for the ball, Saints backup cornerback Chris Reis covered it. Reis's job on the play was to stay back and make sure no Colt returned the kick for a touchdown. But when the ball popped to him, he pounced. Reis then spent more than a minute at the bottom of the pile trying to hang on as Colts attempted to take the ball back.

New Orleans rode the momentum of the ambush kickoff to a 27–17 victory. Morstead spent 10 more seasons with the Saints. Reis never played another NFL game. Both left the team having made a huge impact on the Saints' first Super Bowl win.

A HEALING PLAY

Chris Reis's onside kick recovery did more than help the Saints win the Super Bowl. It may have saved his father's life. Mike Reis had struggled with addiction issues for years. After the Super Bowl, he told Chris that the play inspired him to get help. The two eventually wrote a book called "Recovery of a Lifetime." They also toured the country together speaking to people battling addiction.

Chris Reis appeared in two playoff games for the Saints after the 2009 season without recording a defensive statistic. But his onside kick recovery was one of the biggest plays of the postseason.

HONORABLE MENTIONS

SUPER BOWL XVIII JANUARY 22, 1984

Second-year linebacker Jack Squirek started only one game all season for the Los Angeles Raiders. But his 5-yard interception return for a touchdown with 12 seconds left in the first half was a huge play against Washington. The score made the game 21–3 in Los Angeles's favor. Washington never recovered as the Raiders won 38–9.

SUPER BOWL XXV JANUARY 27, 1991

New York Giants quarterback Jeff Hostetler took over in the playoffs for the injured Phil Simms. Hostetler had been thinking about retiring before he got his chance. But his tough play against a fierce Buffalo Bills' pass rush helped New York eke out a 20–19 victory in the January 1991 game. The game revived his career, and Hostetler played seven more NFL seasons with three teams.

SUPER BOWL XXVIII JANUARY 30, 1994

Dallas Cowboys cornerback James Washington scooped a fumble by Buffalo Bills running back Thurman Thomas early in the third quarter. Washington then raced 48 yards for a score. Before the play, the Bills had led 13–6. Dallas went on to win 30–13. In addition to that big moment, Washington also had an interception on the first play of the fourth quarter that led to another Dallas touchdown.

Jeff Hostetler

Deion Branch

SUPER BOWL XXXIV

JANUARY 30, 2000

Journeyman linebacker Mike Jones spent 12 seasons with four NFL teams. Playing for the St. Louis Rams in 1999, he cemented his legacy. Jones stopped Tennessee Titans wide receiver Kevin Dyson at the 1-yard line on the game's final play to seal a 23–16 win for the Rams.

SUPER BOWL XXXIX FEBRUARY 6, 2005

New England Patriots' receiver Deion Branch had a knack for stepping up big in Super Bowl games. In Super Bowl XXXVIII after the 2003 season, he caught 10 passes for 143 yards and a score against the Carolina Panthers. A year later, the Philadelphia Eagles couldn't stop him either. Branch tied a Super Bowl record with 11 catches for 133 yards. He didn't find the end zone. But he did walk away as the game's MVP.

SUPER BOWL LIV FEBRUARY 2, 2020

Kansas City Chiefs running back Damian Williams caught the go-ahead touchdown with 2:44 left against the San Francisco 49ers in the February 2020 game. He then scored another touchdown with 1:12 left to put the game away. He finished with 104 rushing yards. That made him just the third running back since 2010 to go over 100 yards in a Super Bowl game.

GLOSSARY

contention
Involvement in a race for a championship.

curfew
An hour of night after which players must stay home.

draft
A system that allows teams to acquire new players coming into a league.

expansion
The addition of new teams to increase the size of a league.

journeyman
A player who has played for many teams or has been unable to find a specific role.

legacy
Something of importance that came from someone in the past.

offensive coordinator
A football coach who is in charge of the team's offense, and often calls each play.

onside kick
A kickoff that is purposely short with the hope that the kicking team can recover the ball.

postseason
Another word for playoffs; the time after the end of the regular season when teams play to determine a champion.

secondary
The defensive players—cornerbacks and safeties—who start the play farthest from the line of scrimmage.

special teams
The players on the field for kicking and punting plays.

two-point conversion
An option for teams that have scored a touchdown to try a running or passing play from the 2-yard line for two points, instead of kicking for one point.

MORE INFORMATION

Books

Graves, Will. *GOATs of Football*. Abdo, 2022

Hanlon, Luke. *Football Strategies*. Abdo, 2024.

Stathes, Corbu. *Everything Football*. Abdo, 2025.

Online Resources

Booklinks
NONFICTION NETWORK
FREE! ONLINE NONFICTION RESOURCES

To learn more about surprise Super Bowl heroes, please visit **abdobooklinks.com** or scan this QR code. These links are routinely monitored and updated to provide the most current information available.

INDEX

Bolton, Nick, 20
Bradshaw, Terry, 8
Brady, Tom, 13–14, 31, 38
Brooks, Derrick, 22
Brown, Larry, 21
Brown, Willie, 37–38

Clark, Gary, 8
Curtis, Mike, 27

Foles, Nick, 13–14

Gannon, Rich, 21–23
Griese, Bob, 8

Howard, Desmond, 28–30
Howley, Chuck, 17

Jackson, Dexter, 22–23
Jaworski, Ron, 18, 20
Jones, Ed "Too Tall," 18
Jones, Jacoby, 32, 34–35

Manning, Eli, 40
Manning, Peyton, 24
Martin, Curtis, 29
Martin, Harvey, 17–18
Martin, Rod, 18, 20
McGee, Max, 5–6
Monk, Art, 8
Montana, Joe, 10
Morstead, Thomas, 42

Namath, Joe, 6–7

O'Brien, Jim, 27–28

Plunkett, Jim, 7–8
Pugh, Jethro, 18

Reis, Chris, 42
Rice, Jerry, 10

Sanders, Deion, 21
Sanders, Ricky, 8–10
Smith, Dwight, 22–23
Smith, Malcolm, 23–24
Smith, Timmy, 8, 10–11
Snell, Matt, 7
Starr, Bart, 5, 8
Staubach, Roger, 8

Taylor, John, 10
Tyree, David, 40

Vinatieri, Adam, 30–32
Vrabel, Mike, 38, 40

Wagner, Bobby, 23
Wentz, Carson, 14
White, James, 13
White, Randy, 18
Williams, Doug, 8, 10
Wilson, Marc, 8
Wright, K. J., 23

About the Author

David J. Clarke is a freelance sportswriter. Originally from Helena, Montana, he now lives in Savannah, Georgia.